MARK McGWIRE

By Alan Schwarz

A SPORTS ILLUSTRATED FOR KIDS Book

Head to Head Baseball: Mark McGwire, by Alan Schwarz;
Sammy Sosa, by Michael Bradley
A SPORTS ILLUSTRATED FOR KIDS publication/March 2000

SPORTS ILLUSTRATED FOR KIDS and [KIDS] are registered trademarks of
Time Inc.

Cover and interior design by Nina Gaskin
Cover photographs by John Iacono/SPORTS ILLUSTRATED (Mark
McGwire), Stephen Green/SPORTS ILLUSTRATED (Sammy Sosa)

Head to Head Baseball: Mark McGwire and *Sammy Sosa* is published by
SPORTS ILLUSTRATED FOR KIDS, a division of Time Inc. Its trademark is
registered in the U.S. Patent and Trademark Office and in other
countries. SPORTS ILLUSTRATED FOR KIDS, 1271 Avenue of the Americas,
New York, N.Y. 10020

For information, address: SPORTS ILLUSTRATED FOR KIDS

ISBN 1-886749-89-2

Printed in the United States of America
10 9 8 7 6 5 4 3 2 1

Head to Head Baseball: Mark McGwire and *Sammy Sosa* is a production
of SPORTS ILLUSTRATED FOR KIDS Books:
Cathrine Wolf, Assistant Managing Editor; Emily Peterson Perez, Art
Director; Amy Lennard Goehner (Project Editor) and Margaret Sieck,
Senior Editors; Sherie Holder, Associate Editor; Nina Gaskin, Designer;
Kathleen Fieffe, Reporter; Robert J. Rohr, Copy Editor; Erin Tricarico,
Photo Researcher; Ron Beuzenburg, Production Manager

CONTENTS

1
HOME-RUN KING

It seemed as if the whole world were watching. It was September 8, 1998, and millions of baseball fans were on the edge of their seats. Mark McGwire stepped to the plate at Busch Stadium, in St. Louis, Missouri, in the fourth inning, to face Chicago Cub pitcher Steve Trachsel. Every fan in the ballpark was cheering.

Camera flashes started popping like fireworks as the pitch neared the plate. Fans were hoping that Mark would tag Steve for one more.

Mark had tied Roger Maris's single-season home-run record just the day before. Roger's record of 61 homers had stood for 37 years. Roger died in 1985, but his wife and kids were at the game, in a row of seats near the St. Louis dugout. They wanted to see this piece of history, too.

Mark swung. Most of his home runs had been long, towering fly balls. This time he hit a wicked line drive. In an instant, the ball rocketed into the leftfield stands. The crowd let out a roar, and fans in the leftfield section made a mad scramble for the ball.

When Mark rounded first base, he had a look of pure

joy and wonder in his eyes. His teammates leaped from the dugout. Cub first baseman Mark Grace shook his hand. When Mark crossed home plate, he made a beeline for his 10-year-old son, Matt. He lifted Matt into the air, gently put him down, and climbed into the stands to hug the Maris family. He had done it! He had hit his 62nd home run of the season!

He keeps going and going and going . . .

But Mark wasn't finished hitting home runs. He didn't just break Roger's record — he went on to shatter it. Mark wound up hitting 70 home runs that season —70! — and hit another 65 the next season. And he showed no signs of stopping. Through 1999, Mark averaged one major league home run for every 10.8 times at bat. Not even Babe Ruth hit the long ball more often. Nor as far. Some of Mark's homers have traveled more than 500 feet. That's almost equal to the distance of two football fields! In 1998, against the Florida Marlins at Busch Stadium, he smashed a ball into a grandstand advertising sign that was 545 feet away. The sign was later patched with a giant Band-Aid and the word *Ouch!*

Mark has hit 50 or more home runs in four straight seasons, another first. He has become a legend before our very eyes.

Mark is so strong and has such a short, powerful

swing that he makes hitting home runs look easy. It isn't, of course. "It's not like the pitcher puts the ball on a tee and says, 'Here, Mark, hit it as far as you can,' " Mark once said. "Hitting a home run is probably the hardest thing to do in sports."

The truth is, nothing in Mark's career has come easily. He has faced plenty of obstacles. His eyesight is so poor that since Little League he has needed glasses just to see ground balls. Until college, coaches looked at him more as a pitcher than a hitter. He hit so poorly in his first season in the minor leagues that he nearly quit baseball. In 1991, he batted just .201. Several years later, after a series of discouraging injuries, Mark considered quitting again. He learned that it wasn't enough to be big and strong. Success, he came to realize, took intelligence, hard work, and confidence, too.

Now the best hitters in the game are Mark McGwire fans. Said eight-time batting champion Tony Gwynn of the San Diego Padres: "His swing is so nice and easy. It teaches a valuable lesson: You don't have to swing hard to hit the ball a long way."

Heart of gold

Mark is rough on baseballs and opposing pitchers, but off the field, he's a gentle giant. He spends a lot of time with his son, Matt, who is the bat boy for the Cards. Mark says that everything he does in life and in baseball now is for his son. He signs tons of autographs for fans and is humble about his success.

Baseball's supreme slugger spends much of his spare time raising money for disadvantaged kids. He donates $1 million per year to the Mark McGwire Foundation for Children, which helps abused children in St. Louis and Southern California. When talking about the difficulties of mistreated children, Mark becomes so emotional, he sometimes cries.

Perhaps the reason he's so drawn to kids is that there is still some kid left in Mark. He hasn't forgotten his own childhood years, when he was a shy Southern California kid who lived to play baseball. Even though playing ball is now Mark's job, his approach to the game has stayed the same. He loves the challenge of figuring out a pitcher, then tattooing him for a home run. He loves the teamwork that goes into winning. He loves to joke around with other ballplayers, especially with his main home-run rival, "Slammin' " Sammy Sosa of the Chicago Cubs. Though Mark makes millions of dollars a year playing baseball, money isn't the most important thing to him. He plays the game because it's fun.

"I love to play," Mark said. "I wish I'd hear more players say that. This is a kid's game. There are millions of kids who'd love to be in our shoes."

Sometimes, Mark thinks about his accomplishments and pinches himself. He is one of only 16 players in history to hit more than 500 home runs, and all but one of those players are in baseball's Hall of Fame.

"What I've done blows me away. I say to myself, 'You've got to be kidding me. Have I really done that?' "

He sure has.

2 CALIFORNIA KID

Mark David McGwire was born on October 1, 1963, in Pomona, California. He was the third of five brothers, all of whom grew to be at least 6' 3" tall. Mark, Mike, Bob, Dan, and J.J. had such big appetites that their mother, Ginger McGwire, had to triple most recipes. Dan grew to be the tallest, at 6' 8".

Mark wasn't the only athlete in the family. Dan was a star college quarterback who played five years in the National Football League. Mike played high school golf and soccer. Bob played golf in college. Ginger grew up playing tennis, volleyball, and golf.

Mark's dad, John, was perhaps the most amazing of all the McGwire athletes. As a boy, Mr. McGwire suffered from

COURTESY OF THE McGWIRE FAMILY

Mark at age 10

polio, a crippling disease that left him with one leg much shorter than the other. Even so, he boxed in college and became an excellent golfer. Once, he rode a bicycle all the way from San Francisco, California, to Santa Barbara, California. That's more than 300 miles! He became a dentist and settled down with his wife and five children in Southern California.

Mark and his brothers grew up in the small town of Claremont, California, an hour's drive from Los Angeles. From an early age, it was clear that Mark was a good athlete. He joined the Little League when he was 8 and hit a home run in his very first at-bat! He hit 13 homers that season, a Claremont record.

Mark became one of the town's top athletes. But you'd never know it from the way he acted. He was shy, the kind of boy who liked to sit in the back of the room and just blend in, he told *Sports Illustrated.* "I was always just a basic athlete, nothing extraordinary. But I was a hard worker. And I liked to do a lot of that work where people couldn't see me. I'd throw balls against a cement wall or set a ball on a tee and hit it."

If anything, Mark was embarrassed by his success. Instead of displaying his sports trophies, he stashed them in his closet.

He was generous to a fault. Often, he'd give away his belongings to friends: shirts, sweaters, baseball gloves. Once, he even donated his shoes to a friend. "I gave them to Stan. He needed them," he told his mom when she asked where his shoes were.

Mark enrolled at Damien High School, a Catholic boys' school in nearby La Verne, California. One of his English teachers, Dick Larson, recalls Mark fondly: "He was very much a regular kid, well-liked by other students and not regarded as a star athlete," said Mr. Larson in the book *Mark McGwire: Home Run Hero*.

During his freshman year at Damien, Mark almost quit baseball. While playing for the junior varsity, he pulled a muscle in his chest and switched to the golf team. He seemed to lose interest in baseball and decided to concentrate on golf instead. He led his new teammates to the area championship. (Today, Mark can hit a golf ball as far as Tiger Woods — a whopping 350 yards!)

Mark McGwire — on the mound!

But Mark realized he missed baseball. The following spring, he joined the high school varsity team. Mark was already 6' 5" and had bright red hair. His classmates nicknamed him "Tree." Around school, his home runs became the stuff of legend. One of his foul balls cleared a fence 320 feet away, carried over a soccer field, and bounced once before going through an open door to the school gym. It traveled more than 500 feet.

Even so, Tom Carroll, Mark's coach, considered him primarily a pitcher. It wasn't hard to see why. Mark threw

89 miles per hour. That's as fast as the average big-league pitcher. Plus, he had good control. During a summer tournament in Laramie, Wyoming, Mark pitched a no-hitter to lead his American Legion team to the championship.

"His whole thing was, he scared the other kids," Tom told the St. Louis *Post-Dispatch*. "He had that high leg kick and that long stride. He made it look like he was nearly stepping on home plate as he was releasing the baseball."

Off to college

By 1981, his senior year, Mark was Damien's star pitcher. His 5–3 record was misleading. Baseball scouts and college recruiters drooled over his strikeout totals and his microscopic 1.90 earned run average. They cared less that Mark was also the team's best hitter, combining power with a .359 batting average.

The Montreal Expos were so impressed by his fastball, his character, and his appetite for hard work that they made Mark their eighth-round draft pick. Mark had dreamed of this moment. But when the Expos offered him just a small bonus to sign a minor league contract, Mark decided to attend the University of Southern California instead.

"I had never thought of going to college, because I didn't think I would enjoy it," Mark said in

Mark McGwire: Home Run Hero. "That was one of the best decisions I ever made."

That August, Mark left Claremont for Southern Cal, in Los Angeles. He still thought of himself as a pitcher. But that would soon change.

START OF SOMETHING BIG

When Mark arrived at the University of Southern California in the fall of 1981, he wasn't dreaming of hitting tape-measure home runs for the Trojans. "I wanted to be a pitcher," Mark said. Despite his enormous strength, he thought of himself as a pitcher first.

The University of Southern California (also called USC) is known for its championship baseball teams. Pitchers Randy Johnson and Hall-of-Famer Tom Seaver are two of its more famous players. So Mark wasn't surprised when he didn't play much his freshman year, 1982. He pitched in 20 games and did pretty well. He had a 4–4 record and a 3.04 ERA. But he struggled at the plate. He batted .200, with just three home runs in 75 at-bats.

Batting practice was a different story, though. Because Mark didn't have to think about pitching, he could focus on hitting. He blasted home run after home run. Ron Vaughn, a USC assistant coach, began to wonder what the big redhead might accomplish if he put his full concentration into hitting. During the summers, Ron helped coach the Anchorage Glacier Pilots, an amateur-league team in Alaska. He arranged for Mark to play with the team after his freshman season at USC.

Mark went, but he wasn't happy. He was 2,400 miles from home, and he missed his family. "I was away from home for the first time in my life, with a group of people I didn't know," Mark said. "I went through a very bad period of homesickness."

Mark told his dad that he wanted to come home, but his dad said to stick it out. It was a good thing he did. Coach Vaughn worked with Mark on his swing every day in the batting cage. He told Mark about all the great players who had started as pitchers and developed into fearsome sluggers — players such as Dave Winfield (465 career home runs), Dave Kingman (442 career home runs), and the greatest of all, Babe Ruth (714 career home runs). Eventually, Mark got used to his new surroundings and was able to concentrate on his hitting.

By the end of the summer, Mark had developed into the most powerful hitter in the league. He whacked 13 homers, drove in 53 runs, and led his team with a .403 average.

When Mark returned to USC that fall, he told head coach Rod Dedeaux that he wanted to concentrate solely on hitting. Mark pitched in just eight games that season, finishing 3–1 with an excellent 2.78 ERA. But the plate was where he really shone. Mark blasted 19 home runs, a USC record. Still, he had barely tapped his potential.

That season, Coach Dedeaux said, "Mark was really just learning. He'd swing at a lot of bad balls. Patience is what he needed more than anything else."

In 1984, Mark's junior year, he showed just how good he could be. He blasted 32 home runs, more than anyone else in college baseball that year. That gave him 54 career home runs — another USC record. He was a first-team All-America, and *The Sporting News* named him the College Player of the Year.

Major league scouts were well aware of his feats. The New York Mets had the Number 1 pick in the June baseball draft, and they wanted to take him. But the team

JACQUELINE DUVOISIN/SPORTS ILLUSTRATED

Mark at the 1984 Olympics

changed its mind when it heard Mark's contract demands. The Oakland Athletics selected Mark with the 10th pick in the draft. Mark left college after his junior year. That summer, he played for Team USA, the 1984 U. S Olympic Baseball Team. The Mets would soon realize that Mark was well worth the money it would have cost to sign him.

He began to prove it that summer while playing for Team USA. The team played several exhibition games in major league stadiums. During a game in Boston's Fenway Park, Mark hit a ball against a concrete wall in centerfield, more than 450 feet away. Hall of Fame slugger Reggie Jackson was watching. "My goodness, that's the longest ball I've ever seen hit," Reggie said, in awe.

A shaky start in the minors

Soon after the Olympics, Mark reported to the Modesto [California] A's, an Oakland team in the lower minor leagues. His first games as a professional were disappointing. He batted just .200, with one home run in 16 games. He made many errors and struck out a lot. He played so poorly that he lost all confidence. He even thought about quitting. Kathy Williamson, whom Mark had married in 1984, recalls those dark days. "I can remember lying in bed in the middle of the night and hearing Mark say, 'I can't hit the baseball anymore. I'm done. I've lost it. I've got to quit,' " she said.

But Mark loved baseball too much to walk away.

Mark returned to Modesto in 1985. He had been playing first base. The A's thought he might do better at third base. They were wrong. Once more, he struggled defensively, making 33 errors. But he had had a major breakthrough in his batting after adjusting his hitting stance and moving closer to the plate. He bashed 24 home runs, tying for the league lead, and collected 106 RBIs.

That was good enough to earn Mark a promotion. In 1986, he joined the Huntsville [Alabama] Stars of the Double-A Southern League. He dominated the league from the start, hitting 10 home runs in less than two months. In mid-season, the A's promoted him again, this time to the Tacoma [Washington] Tigers of the Triple-A Pacific Coast League. He hit 13 more homers in just three months.

Moving up to the big time

The call Mark had waited for all his life came on August 20, 1986. Oakland called to tell him he had been promoted to the major leagues! Four days later, Mark got his first major league hit, a single against New York Yankee pitcher Tommy John in Yankee Stadium. Talk about a coincidence — Mark's dad was Tommy's dentist. Tommy joked: "When your dentist's kid starts hitting you, it's time to retire."

Mark hit his first major league home run the following day, off Detroit Tiger pitcher Walt Terrell at Tiger Stadium. It turned out to be one of his few good moments that season in the big leagues. Mark batted just .189 for the season, with only three home runs. Worse, he made six errors in 18 games at third base. That winter, he worried that the A's would send him down to the minors. He had worked hard to get to the majors and had no desire to go back down.

"Getting to the major leagues is one thing," Mark said. "The hardest part is staying there."

4
UPS AND DOWNS WITH THE A'S

Mark wasn't guaranteed a big-league job when spring training began, in February 1987. The A's saw him as a potential slugger. But they were worried about his fielding. He made the team, but as a bench warmer. Mark struggled during the first weeks of the season, batting .167, and again he feared he would be sent down to the minors.

But the A's were weak at first base, and they needed a home-run hitter. Manager Tony La Russa decided to give Mark a chance. He moved Mark to first and promised to play him every day. That was the break Mark needed. Tony's confidence helped Mark believe in himself. He went on to have one of the best rookie seasons ever.

In 1987, Mark hit 49 home runs, to lead the American League. (The previous rookie home-run record had been 38.) That's when the legend of Mark McGwire began.

Mark was so good so fast, his teammates kept coming up with new nicknames for him. They called him "Orange Crunch" because of his red hair. They called him "Marco Solo" because many of his homers were solo shots. Then, of course, there was the nickname "Big Mac" — the one that stuck.

At that season's All-Star Game, which was played in Oakland, California, Mark was the talk of baseball. Few rookies make the All-Star team, but, then, few hit 33 home runs by mid-July. Mark was compared to Roger Maris for the first time. It wouldn't be the last.

After that, Mark's home-run pace slowed. He was one homer short of 50, entering the last day of the season. Fans across the U.S. were rooting for him to hit one more. No player had reached 50 since Cincinnati Red outfielder George Foster blasted 52 home runs in 1977.

Mark skipped the game. In doing so, he earned the nation's love and admiration. Mark's wife, Kathy, was about to give birth to Matt that day in California. Mark flew home to be with her. "I'll never have another first child," Mark said, "but I will have another chance to hit 50 home runs."

It was no surprise when Mark was unanimously selected as the American League Rookie of the Year.

The new "Bash" makes a splash

I n the late 1980's, the A's were the best team in baseball. Starting in 1988, they won three American League championships in a row. Mark wasn't the team's only star. He and slugging outfielder Jose Canseco became known as the "Bash Brothers." They were the most feared home-run-hitting duo in baseball. Future Hall-of-Fame pitcher Dennis Eckersley was also on the team.

In 1988, their second full season together, Jose hit 42 homers and won the American League's Most Valuable Player award. Mark added 32 homers. Some fans were disappointed. They wondered if his total of 49 the year before was a fluke. "Look, I don't think I'll ever hit 40 home runs again," Mark insisted. "I'll be very happy to hit between 25 and 30 every year. Not many guys have done that." That sounds pretty funny, now.

The A's played the Los Angeles Dodgers in the 1988 World Series and lost, four games to one. Oakland's only victory came in Game 3, when Mark hit a home run in the bottom of the ninth inning for a 2–1 win.

Mark hit 33 more home runs in 1989, and helped lead the team back to the World Series. This time, they faced the San Francisco Giants, their rivals from across the San Francisco Bay. (Oakland and San Francisco are neighboring cities along the northern California coast.) The A's swept the Giants in four games. Mark was a world champion.

In 1990, Mark hit 39 home runs and helped lead the A's to their third straight World Series. By then, he was more than just a home-run hitter. He had worked extra hard on his fielding for four years, and that season, his hard work finally paid off. He won the Gold Glove award as the best defensive first baseman in the league. Mighty Mark had become a complete player at last.

Off the field, though, things weren't going so well. Mark's personal life was a mess. He and Kathy were divorced in 1988. He blamed himself for the breakup. He missed Matt terribly. Mark was lonely, and his problems affected his play on the field.

Though Mark kept hitting home runs, his batting average dropped steadily. He struck out a lot. He wasn't happy about anything in his life. The bottom dropped out in 1991. Mark batted only .201 and hit just 22 home runs. Fans at the ballpark booed him. Kids walked by his Alamo, California, home and yelled, "McGwire, you stink!" He tried dozens of different batting stances, to try to break his slump. But nothing worked. Once more, he considered quitting baseball.

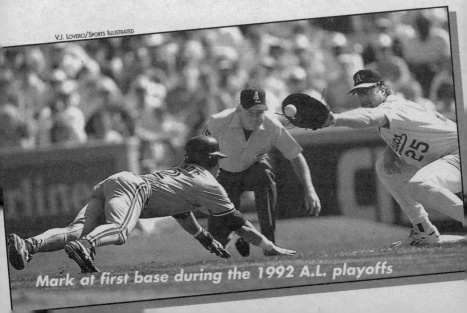

V.J. LOVERO/SPORTS ILLUSTRATED

Mark at first base during the 1992 A.L. playoffs

"Everything went wrong . . . everything," Mark said. "I'm not afraid to admit it. I stunk. It was a big eye-opener. It happens to everybody. I don't care who you are. Down the line, this game of baseball is going to come up and beat you. It kicked me in '91. It woke me up."

One night, he took a long drive by himself and did a lot of thinking. He realized that he was more than unhappy — he was terribly depressed.

A cry for help

Mark knew he needed help to sort out his feelings. He decided to visit a psychologist. (A psychologist *[sigh-COLL-oh-jist]* is a person trained to help others learn to understand their feelings.)

"That was the turning point in my life as a person and as a professional ballplayer," Mark later told *Sport* magazine. "Seeking help made me the person I am today. It made me find out what I'm all about. I believe that anyone who confronts his problems succeeds."

It sure helped Mark. In 1992, he again became one of the top players in the game. He hit 42 home runs — the first time since his rookie season that he had reached 40 — and drove in 104 runs. The Bash Brother had returned!

Unfortunately, he wasn't back for long. Mark missed most of the next two seasons because of injuries. He played in just 74 of Oakland's 322 games in 1993 and 1994.

First, in May 1993, Mark hurt his left heel. Then his back stiffened up. In September, he had surgery to fix his heel. It didn't help. A year later, he had more surgery.

Some players might have grown discouraged and stayed away from the ballpark. Not Mark. He went to every home game and away game. And for the first time, he really studied the game. "I learned how much I loved it," Mark said. "It was the first time in my career that I ever sat back and watched the game of baseball in the dugout for any length of time. I started watching pitchers, I started watching hitters. I learned a tremendous amount."

While Mark sat, people wondered if he would ever fully recover — and if he would ever be great again.

He returned to the lineup in 1995. It didn't take long to find out.

5

BIG MAC
BUSTS LOOSE

Mark's first eight seasons in the big leagues had been a roller-coaster ride. He had been a home-run champion as a rookie. He had suffered through injuries. He had won a World Series. He had seen his personal life fall apart.

His one wish for 1995 was to stay healthy and play a full season of baseball, injury-free. He wanted to see how good he could be.

He didn't quite get that chance. Mark played in just 104 games, because of injuries and the players' strike that ended the season. But what he accomplished in those 104 games was mind-boggling! In two days in June, against the Boston Red Sox, he hit five home runs. He went on a torrid streak just before the strike, hitting 11 homers in 18 games.

Mark finished the season with 39 home runs in 317 at-bats. That's an average of one homer for every 8.13 at-bats, or about one homer every two games. No one in history, not Hank Aaron, not Roger Maris, not even the great Babe Ruth, had hit home runs that frequently. Mark seemed poised to have another monster season in 1996.

But foot injuries struck again. Mark missed another 32 ball games in '96. Once again, he grew so discouraged that he thought about retiring. Then he remembered his father and all that he had achieved despite the pain he had suffered from polio. "My injuries are meaningless compared to what my father went through," Mark said in 1997. Mark made up his mind to get back on the field.

Hitting the long ball

Once he did, he caught fire. And he stayed hot the entire season. Starting on May 17, Mark hit 21 home runs in 36 games. On June 25, against the Detroit Tigers, he hit career homer number 300.

Not only was Mark hitting homers often, he was hitting them so much farther than people had ever seen before.

During this time, Mark added 25 pounds of muscle to his body by lifting weights. He trained with his brother J.J., who wanted to become a pro body builder. Mark also began doing eye exercises to help him see the ball better, and he adjusted his batting stance.

On July 24, against the White Sox, he blasted a 470-foot homer — the longest by a visiting player — in Chicago's new Comiskey Park. The next day, in Toronto, he hammered a pitch into the fifth deck at SkyDome.

The ball sailed an unbelievable 488 feet, a ballpark record.

Mark never slowed down. On September 14, against the Cleveland Indians, he hit home run number 50. That was a special event for Mark. Nine years earlier, he had skipped the chance to reach 50 so that he could be present at his son Matt's birth. Remembering that, Mark gave the home-run ball to Matt as a special souvenir. He finished the season with 52 homers, leading the major leagues and setting an Oakland record. He scored 104 runs, had 113 RBIs, and walked 116 times. He also batted .312. He had become a well-rounded hitter.

By 1997, when Big Mac stepped to the plate, fans stopped talking. Hot-dog vendors stopped selling franks. Opposing players were no different. They wanted to see what Big Mac was going to do, too. "Even I'm wondering when he's going to hit another bomb," said Chuck Knoblauch, then the second baseman for the Minnesota Twins.

On April 20, Mark hit a 514-foot bomb that cleared the leftfield roof at Tiger Stadium. Ten days later, in Cleveland, he hit a ball so hard that it dented an advertising sign on the scoreboard high above left-centerfield.

Then, on June 24, he faced the Seattle Mariners' Randy Johnson, the hardest thrower in baseball. *Boom!* Mark slammed Randy's 97-m.p.h. fastball a whopping 538 feet into the upper deck in Seattle's Kingdome, just six rows from the back of the stands. It was the longest home run since baseball officially began measuring home-run distances, in 1992. Not even the other players could believe it. Outfielder Steve Finley, then with the San Diego Padres, said it best: "The rest of us shoot for the front row. But Mark shoots for the back row!"

As always, Mark remained modest about his ability. "I try not to swing too hard," he said. "I have a natural lift. That's the player I am."

Mark had become one of the greatest players in the game and one of the best home-run hitters ever. He was on his way toward topping 50 home runs for the second straight season, something only Babe Ruth had done. For the ninth time, he was selected to the All-Star team. It seemed unimaginable that a team would trade away such a superstar.

St. Louis rolls out the welcome mat

Oakland was in a bind. Mark was going to be a free agent after the season, and the A's weren't sure they could afford to pay him what he deserved. So they decided to trade him for a group of younger players.

Mark had hoped to sign with the Los Angeles Dodgers or the Anaheim Angels so that he could stay close to Matt. Instead, the A's traded him to the St. Louis Cardinals, on July 31, 1997, for pitchers Eric Ludwick, T.J. Mathews, and Blake Stein. Mark wasn't sure how to feel. He never had played in the National League. And he was a long way from Matt and home in California.

Fortunately, there was one familiar face. Tony La Russa, the manager who had given Mark the chance to play as a rookie in Oakland, was now managing the Cardinals. Mark was thrilled to be reunited with Tony. He was willing to give St. Louis a chance.

It didn't take long for Cardinal fans to fall in love with Mark. And Mark soon fell in love with the fans, the team, and the city. On September 16, 1997, he signed a three-year contract worth at least $30 million and announced that he was starting a foundation to care for abused kids. He pledged to donate $1 million a year for three years to help get it started. Mark broke down in tears when he talked to reporters about the project. Over the years, the many stories he had heard of mistreated children had remained in his heart. Now, at last, he had enough money to do something about it.

The contract had one other provision. Mark asked the Cardinals to give Matt a guaranteed seat on any team charter flight. They agreed. "I made them well aware that he's the most important thing in my life," Mark said.

The day Mark signed his Cardinal contract, he not only won hearts, he made history. That night, against the Los Angeles Dodgers in St. Louis's Busch Stadium, he hit a 517-foot home run, the longest homer in that stadium's history. The next time Mark came to the plate, he received a standing ovation that lasted through his entire at-bat.

"I still remember that night," Mark said. "It will always be in my memory bank. I was definitely floating. It was an absolutely tremendous feeling."

Was 61 possible?

Mark had hit 34 home runs with the A's in 1997. He added 24 with the Cardinals that season. That made a total of 58, which tied him with Hank Greenberg for the most homers by a right-handed hitter in a single season. (Hank hit 58 while playing for the Detroit Tigers in 1938.) Only Mark and Babe Ruth had hit 50 or more home runs in consecutive seasons.

Fifty-eight was remarkable. But could Mark top Roger Maris's 61? All winter, that was all any baseball fan — or baseball player — could talk about. It was the first question reporters asked Mark when he arrived at spring training in 1998. Everyone wanted to know.

"Can it be done?" Mark asked. "Yes. When? I don't know. It would have to be a perfect year."

C6 A HOME-RUN RACE FOR THE AGES

Mark felt that to break Roger Maris's record, he'd have to start his home-run charge on Opening Day. That's just what he did. He homered in each of the Cardinals' first four games of 1998. The first was against the Los Angeles Dodgers, and it was no ordinary blast — it was a grand slam! The last player to start the season with

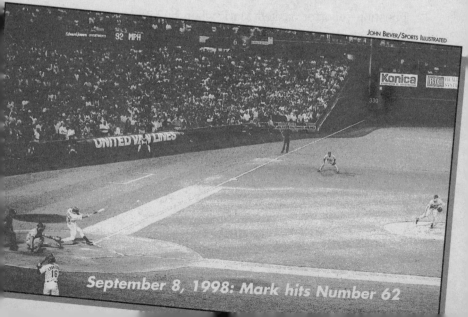

JOHN BIEVER/SPORTS ILLUSTRATED

September 8, 1998: Mark hits Number 62

such a streak was the great Willie Mays, who did it in 1971.

All around Mark, people were tingling with excitement. Teammates, and opponents, too, spoke of him with awe. Already, reporters were crowding around him before and after games, wanting Mark to talk about Roger Maris and the record.

Mark tried to play down his hot start. He knew he had a long way to go. Deep down, he wasn't sure if people really wanted to see the record broken — by anyone. Many baseball fans had not supported Roger as he approached Babe Ruth's record, in 1961.

The Babe had been the greatest, most beloved player in the history of baseball. Roger had been neither great nor beloved. He was a very good player having a magical season. In fact, it was the only season in which he hit more than 39 home runs. People rooted against him because they didn't think he deserved to break Babe's record. Would they think the same of Mark? Would he be able to handle all the media pressure? Mark wasn't sure. So he tried to play down the home-run chase when he talked to reporters.

"There's absolutely no basis to even talk about [the record] until somebody is close to 50 by September," he told reporters, over and over. But they kept asking.

On April 14, Mark hit three homers in a game against the Arizona Diamondbacks. That gave him seven in 13 games. The reporters pressed him about his run at the record, but Mark was determined to stay low key. His son, Matt, had served as the Cardinals' bat boy that day, which made those homers even more special to Mark.

On May 8, he clouted career home-run number 400, against New York Met pitcher Rick Reed. It was a typical Mark mega-blast. "I didn't think it would ever come down," Rick told reporters after the game. Mark had reached 400 homers in 4,726 at-bats, faster than anyone in history. Babe had needed 128 more at-bats.

Hey, Mark, meet Sammy!

Mark's homers kept soaring out of stadiums. Number 401 came four days after the 400th — a 527-foot, upper-deck moon shot at Busch Stadium against the Milwaukee Brewers. Mark hammered 14 more long balls in the next 19 days. One was a 545-foot blast against the Florida Marlins. By May 31, he had 27 home runs.

Soon, thousands of fans started arriving at Busch Stadium hours early, just to see Mark warm up. Each day in pre-game batting practice, Mark would hit as many as 10 home runs in 10 minutes. The balls would just soar out of the ballpark.

Mark didn't know what to make of all the attention. He started to feel the pressure to perform. "To do what people expect day in and day out is not an easy task," he said. "It's stressful. I mean, people applaud you when you walk into the [batting] cage. They boo when you bunt. It's unreal. The thing is, I never try to swing hard. I try to work on the same stroke I use in games."

Despite the craziness building around him, Mark stayed focused. He hit 10 home runs in June, to give him 37. He was on a pace to hit 74 home runs for the season, a total that seemed unimaginable. Nearly as unimaginable, he wasn't alone! Another slugger was just four home runs behind him — Chicago Cub rightfielder, "Slammin' " Sammy Sosa.

Sammy once hit 40 home runs 1996. But he had never seemed capable of hitting more, and 1998 didn't seem any different. On May 31, he had a modest 13 homers. Then he went on a streak that almost defied belief. Sammy hit 20 home runs in June, the biggest one-month total in the history of baseball. That gave him 33 homers in just 82 games.

Suddenly, Mark wasn't just chasing Roger. He was trying to beat Sammy, too. The Great Home Run Race of 1998 had begun.

On August 10, Sammy hit home-run number 46 to tie Mark. Mark pulled ahead with a homer of his own the next day. Then on August 19, Sammy hit one against the Cardinals and pulled ahead of Mark for the first time, to lead 48–47. Mark answered with two homers just 57 minutes later. When the game ended, Mark was up, 49–48.

The two sluggers became friends as the season went

on. Mark said of Sammy, "I root him on like everybody else." Sammy answered by saying, "Mark is The Man. I am happy to be behind Mark McGwire." But that did not stop the two from competing.

Their tie didn't last long. Mark crushed number 50 the following day against the Mets. That one made history. Mark was now the only player to hit 50 or more homers in a season three seasons in a row. As he rounded the bases, he raised a fist into the air and clapped his hands twice. Said his manager, Tony La Russa, "Never have I seen him show more emotion than that on the field, and I've seen him hit a home run to win a World Series game."

Mark pulls ahead

Mark had reached 50 on August 20. Once again, reporters asked him about Roger's record. This time, he smiled and told the reporters, "I have to admit I have a shot."

But so did Sammy. They kept jockeying for the lead, like two horses on a racetrack. Then Mark hit home runs on consecutive days, September 1 and 2, to pull ahead by two. He had 59. One more, and he would tie the Babe. Two more, and he'd reach Roger. Three more, and he would stand alone as the all-time home-run king!

The entire country was buzzing. From then on, on orders from baseball commissioner Bud Selig, specially marked balls were to be used whenever Mark or Sammy came to the plate. The commissioner wanted to be sure they would know which ball was used to break the record.

The other ballplayers were in awe. "What [Mark's] doing is amazing," said Pittsburgh Pirate catcher Jason Kendall. "I hope he breaks it, just not against us. No, wait — I'd like to see that!"

On September 5, at home against the Cincinnati Reds, Mark hit number 60. He had tied the Babe! After the game, Mark told reporters, "I wish I could go back in time and meet him."

Two days later, Sammy and the Chicago Cubs came to St. Louis. Mark still had 60 homers. He had a strong feeling, though, that he would tie Roger's record that day. After all, it was September 7, Mark's dad's birthday — his dad was turning 61! The night before, at dinner, Mark had said to him, "Wouldn't it be something if I did it then?" His dad had answered, "If I can do 61 years, you can do 61 homers."

The whole world was watching

It didn't take long for Mark to deliver. He faced Cub pitcher Mike Morgan in the first inning, and slammed a fastball 430 feet down the leftfield line for a home run. Sixty-one! After all Mark had been through, all the questions and all the pressure, he had tied Roger at last. As Mark rounded the bases, Sammy stood in rightfield clapping. When Mark touched home plate, he pointed to his father in the stands and yelled, "Happy birthday, Dad!" One more to go.

Mark awoke the next morning with a stomach ache. But he had a game to play that night, and fans everywhere would be watching. He got out of bed. He went to lunch with friend and teammate Pat Kelly. They had cheese pizza. That was their lucky meal.

When Mark arrived at Busch Stadium that afternoon, the atmosphere was electric. It seemed as if there were reporters and television cameras everywhere he turned. He looked in the stands down the first-base line, near the dugout. Roger Maris's wife and five of their children were seated there. They wanted to witness the moment when Roger's record was broken.

Mark came to bat in the first inning. There were 43,688 fans in the ballpark, and their cheers thundered through the stadium. Mark grounded out to the shortstop.

An hour later, in the fourth inning, he came up again. Cub pitcher Steve Trachsel started him off with a fastball, down and inside. As Mark swung, thousands of flashbulbs lit up the stadium. He hammered a line drive that curled toward the leftfield corner. Would it make it over the fence? Would it stay fair?

Mark ran toward first base, watching and rooting, just like the fans in the stands.

"The next thing I knew, the ball disappeared," Mark

said afterward. "I was in shock. I was numb. I did it! I had all these things running through my mind, and I was just floating in outer space."

The crowd went bananas. Mark was so excited, he bounded over first base without stepping on the bag. He had to turn back and touch it. He jogged around the bases, a smile spreading across his face. The entire Cardinal team met him at home plate. He high-fived them all. Sammy ran in from rightfield, and Mark hugged him, too. "I wanted to congratulate Mark," said Sammy, "because he's my friend." Then Mark turned to his son, Matt, who was serving as the bat boy that day. Mark hoisted him high into the air and held him tight. Then he climbed into the stands and embraced the Maris family.

Miracle worker

After the game, Mark was overcome with emotion. "I have amazed myself," he said. "I have surpassed anything I ever expected of myself in this game."

Still, he had work to do. Mark may have set the major league home-run record, but he hadn't yet won the 1998 home-run race. There were still three weeks left in the season, and Sammy was right on Mark's tail.

Mark went a week without hitting another homer, and Sammy tied him at 62. There were two weeks to go. Mark moved ahead, again. But then Sammy got hot. On September 24, they were tied at 65. The next day, Sammy hit number 66 to take the lead. Hours later, Mark tied him.

Now Mark had two more games left in the season and Sammy had three. Sammy didn't homer in any of the Cub games. He ended up with 66. But Mark wasn't through performing miracles. Against the Montreal Expos, he hit two homers on Saturday and two on Sunday. His last blast gave him 70 homers for the season. Mark had hit five home runs with his last 19 swings. He hadn't merely broken Roger's record, he had *demolished* it.

"I'm in awe of myself right now," Mark said to reporters after hitting number 70. "I can't believe I did it. Can you?"

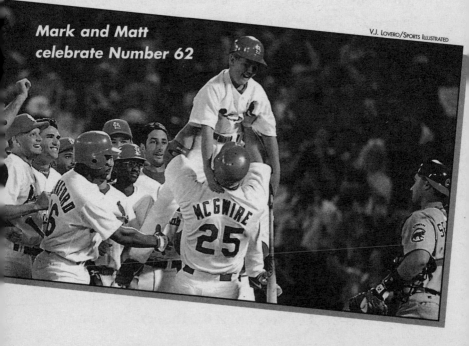

Mark and Matt celebrate Number 62

V.J. Lovero/Sports Illustrated

7
HERE WE GO AGAIN!

On the first day of spring training in 1999, dozens of reporters surrounded Mark. They all wanted to know the same thing. The *entire country* wanted to know: Could he hit 70 home runs again?

To be honest, Mark wasn't sure. But he was certain of one thing — doing it once was hard enough. He wasn't about to put pressure on himself again. His plan was simply not to talk about 1998. "I don't re-live anything," he said. "This is a new year. Last year is historical. It's over with."

At first, it seemed unlikely he would even come close to what he did in 1998. Mark got off to a slow start, hitting just five homers in April. His back was bothering him, and he developed a nasty infection between two toes of his right foot. But he kept playing. By late May, when the Cardinals traveled to Chicago to face the Cubs, he had 14 homers. His friendly rival, Sammy Sosa, had 16. The two met on the field and hugged before the first game of the three-game series.

Sammy homered in the first game. Mark matched him in the last game. That gave Mark 15 homers — still two fewer than Sammy and nine fewer than he'd had at the same point in 1998. Mark was on a pace to reach 50 homers for a record-setting fourth straight season. But his teammates worried that his expectations were too high, that the pressure of achieving was getting to him.

"I think he's been pressing a little bit," Cardinal pitcher Kent Mercker said. "It's only natural. People expect him to [break the record] all over again. He's on pace for 50 home runs. What's wrong with that? Is that a bad year? Come on."

Mark conquers The Green Monster

After May, Mark revved up and picked up the pace. He hit eight more homers in June, then five in the first 10 days of July. By the All-Star break, he was up to 28, second in the league to Sammy's 32.

Fans — and players — had been anticipating the All-Star Home Run Derby that was to take place on the evening before the All-Star Game. That season, the event took place at Boston's Fenway Park and featured such sluggers as Mark, Sammy, and Ken Griffey, Junior. Mark hits most of his home runs to leftfield, and Fenway Park's leftfield wall — which is called The Green Monster — is 37-feet-high, but a short 310 feet from home plate. Fans and players wanted to see how many homers Mark could hit over The Green Monster.

It didn't take long to find out. In the first round, Mark

started shooting balls that easily cleared The Green Monster — *boom, boom, boom*. One ball hit the top of a light tower 470 feet away. Four others traveled even farther. Fans were going crazy. So were the players. Boston Red Sox pitcher Pedro Martinez jokingly ran onto the field and tried to steal Mark's bat. He was convinced there was magic in it.

Mark blasted 13 homers in the opening round of the contest, a derby record. Each traveled an average of 438 feet. Strung together, that's more than a mile! Mark was too pooped to hit many more after that. Ken Griffey, Junior, won the event by hitting more, but Mark had stolen the show.

The next night, before the All-Star Game, Mark stood on the Fenway Park infield with baseball great Ted Williams. Both men had been nominated for the All-Century Team that Major League Baseball would choose after the season. Ted played 19 seasons, all for the Red Sox, hitting .344 during his career and 521 home runs. He was the last player to bat .400 in a season, hitting .406 in 1941. Many consider Ted the greatest hitter who ever lived.

Ted, who was 81 years old, spoke to Mark about hitting. Later, when Mark was asked by reporters about his conversation with Ted, Mark's eyes shone. "I'm just happy he knows who I am and that he talked to me," he said.

The All-Star Game seemed to give Mark some added

energy. Back with the Cardinals, he walloped 11 home runs in the last 16 days of July. That gave him 39 for the season. Sammy had 40. Part 2 of The Great Home-Run Race was on.

On August 5, against the San Diego Padres, Mark hit his 500th home run. He reached that milestone faster than any player in history: in 5,487 at-bats. Babe Ruth needed 314 more at-bats. Mark was now one of 15 players with 500 homers. The others, including Hank Aaron, the Babe, and Willie Mays, are already in the Hall of Fame. When asked about his own place in history, Mark was typically humble. "It's odd to hear those Hall of Fame names with my name," Mark said. "Because as a kid growing up, you don't dream about that. You just think about playing ball in your backyard."

Neck-and-neck

All through August, Mark kept hitting homers. Even so, he couldn't quite catch Sammy. On August 22, Mark hit two long balls in a game against the New York Mets. The first one went 502 feet. The second was Mark's 50th of the season, making him the first major leaguer to hit 50 or more homers in four straight seasons. Sammy had 51.

As September began, the two sluggers once again set their sights on 60. By then, both their teams had fallen out of the National League Central Division race. Though Mark didn't like it, reporters began to focus less on the Cardinals and more on Big Mac's powerful swing.

"The message that's being put out there today," he told them, "is that individual statistics are more important than the team. That's wrong." But who could ignore the drama of the home-run race? And this time, it looked as if Mark would lose. With just nine days left in the season, Sammy had 61 homers to Mark's 59.

But then Mark went on a closing tear, just as he had the season before. On September 27, he tied Sammy at 61. The next day, Sammy pulled ahead again. It would be the last time. Sammy finished with 63. Mark hit two in his last two games, to reach 65. It had taken 37 years for a player to hit more than 61 homers in a single season. Now two players had done the "impossible" two seasons in a row.

"To hit 65 still blows me away," Mark told the *St. Louis Post-Dispatch*. "It blows me away what I did last year, when I hit 70. But when you prepare every day, it shows what you can do."

A place among the greats

Mark's final home run of 1999 gave him 522 for his career, moving him past Ted Williams and San Francisco Giant slugger Willie McCovey and into 10th place on the all-time home-run list. After the season, Mark and New York Yankee legend Lou Gehrig were named as the two first basemen on baseball's All-Century Team.

"All this stuff is going to mean a lot to me even more

when I'm retired," Mark said after the season. "The game of baseball doesn't really allow you to think about what you've done, because you have to play tomorrow. I know I've accomplished a lot. But it will truly hit me when I'm retired and I can sit back and look at everything."

There will be time enough for Mark to take it all in. He isn't finished yet!

8

FUTURE HALL-OF-FAMER

Mark was 36 when the 1999 season ended. That's old by baseball standards. Most players his age are beginning to wind down their careers. They don't play as often, and they don't hit as well as they once did. But Mark seems to be an exception. Like the great Henry Aaron, who holds the all-time home-run record, he is actually getting better.

For the last four seasons, Mark has averaged an amazing 61 home runs per season, a historic rate. If he averages 50 per year for the next four seasons, he'll have 722, in 2003, when he's 40. One more good season after that and he'd break the record. Does Mark think he can do it?

"Somebody said I have a shot at 755, Hank Aaron's career record," Mark said. "I think that's too far away for me. I will say this: How high my career total climbs comes down to my health. If I stay healthy like I have the past few years and I put up the numbers that I'm capable of, who knows how many home runs I'll hit?"

Right now, Mark has a guaranteed contract with the Cardinals through 2001. He says he loves both the team and the city, and doesn't want to play anywhere else.

He has already begun to think about his life after baseball. His immediate plan is to take a few years off to spend time with his son, Matt. If all goes according to plan, Matt will be in high school by then. Mark's dream is for the two of them to spend lots of time together during Matt's summer vacations. That will be a first for Mark. He hasn't had a free summer since his own high school days. His summers have always been taken up by playing baseball.

Looking back, and ahead

Eventually, Mark wants to return to the game. He hopes to coach young players, to teach them all he has learned about the sport he loves.

"I think I have a lot to offer young kids who play this game," he said. "I've been on top of the game, I've been on the bottom of the game. I've been injured. I won the World Series. I've lost the World Series. I've been on last-place teams, first-place teams. I've done it. I want to tell it. I want to teach it. I just love the game. I love it so much."

The changes Mark has made in his own life are as impressive as his accomplishments on the field. He learned that you shouldn't be afraid to seek help for a personal problem. From his father, he learned the true meaning of courage. Most important, he worked hard to build a friendship with his ex-wife and her new husband so that the three of them, together, could help raise Matt.

It seems so long ago since that day in 1986 when Mark, then a skinny 22-year-old, stepped into the batter's box at Detroit's Tiger Stadium and blasted his first big-league home run. He spent much of his career chasing legends. And now, all these years later, he has become a legend himself. The ball he hit and the bat he used when he smashed his record-breaking 62nd home run in 1998 are already in the Baseball Hall of Fame, along with the uniform he wore that day. As soon as he becomes eligible, he will almost certainly be elected to the Hall as one of the greatest sluggers of all time.

Jose Canseco, his former Oakland teammate, said it all: "Mark is incredible. No one can stand in his shoes — not Babe Ruth, not anyone. He's in a league of his own."

SAMMY
SOSA

By Michael Bradley

A Sports Illustrated For Kids Book

CONTENTS

A HERO'S WELCOME

The skies were gray and cloudy on October 20, 1998. Rain fell slowly and steadily. But for many citizens of the Dominican Republic, it was the most beautiful day of the year. Sammy Sosa was coming home!

Chicago Cub rightfielder Sammy Sosa was an American baseball hero. During the 1998 season, he had dueled St. Louis Cardinal slugger Mark McGwire in the greatest home-run race in baseball history. Mark won the competition, breaking Roger Maris' single-season record of 61 home runs by hitting 70 of his own. But Sammy's 66 dingers also soared past Roger's mark and helped the Cubs make the playoffs for the first time since 1989. Sammy hit .308 and knocked in 158 runs, and his amazing season was topped off when he was named the National League's Most Valuable Player.

Sammy's return to the Dominican Republic was declared a National Day of Celebration by the president of the country. There was music and dancing. Dominicans painted the number 66 on their cars, in honor of Sammy's 1998 home-run total.

In Sammy's hometown, San Pedro de Macoris, thousands of people waited up to eight hours in the rain for a chance to see Sammy. He spoke to the crowd about his childhood and how hopeless he felt until the world of baseball opened up to him. Finally, he told his admirers about how he wanted to help them.

"Now that I'm here in my country, I have time to go to every corner and *barrio* ["neighborhood"] to see what people need," Sammy said.

Beloved in his two countries

Sammy knows first-hand what people need and how it feels to do without. His father died when he was 7, and his family was very poor. Baseball rules in the Dominican Republic and, like many kids growing up there, Sammy dreamed about playing pro ball someday.

He moved a step closer to that dream when he was 16 and a scout gave him a tryout. A year later, Sammy moved to the U.S. to begin his pro career. In 13 seasons with three teams, he changed from a wild, impatient batter to one of baseball's most feared sluggers.

In 1999, "Slammin' " Sammy picked up where he had left off in 1998. He hit 63 homers, nosing out Mark McGwire in the race to 60 and becoming the first player to hit 60 round-trippers in each of two seasons. "What Sammy did this year is absolutely remarkable," Mark McGwire told SPORTS ILLUSTRATED FOR KIDS magazine. "I tip my hat to him."

The readers of S.I. FOR KIDS tipped their hat to Sammy, too! They voted him the 1999 Athlete of the Year. Sammy, with his 100-watt smile, is a huge favorite with fans everywhere. He blows kisses to the crowd at Wrigley Field in Chicago, Illinois. "I enjoy everything that I do," says Sammy. "I'm happy."

Sammy no longer has to save every penny he makes. The Cubs signed him to a multi-million dollar contract in 1997. He now has enough money to buy his family anything they want. He also has enough money to help people in need.

Sammy reached out to his countrymen after Hurricane Georges ripped through the Dominican Republic, in September 1998.

"This is something that I need to do for my country," Sammy told the *Los Angeles Times*. "It's not about the home-run race anymore . . . it's about human beings . . . The children don't have enough food and water, and they're scared because of everything that happened."

The Sammy Sosa Foundation, which Sammy started, raised more than $250,000 for relief. The foundation also arranged for the delivery of 80,000 pounds of food and water. Sammy encouraged others to contribute to his fund, and many did, including several major leaguers.

No wonder the Dominicans turned out in force on this National Day of Celebration! As the cheers continued, Sammy said what everybody had come to hear: "*Estoy*

orgulloso de ser Dominicano." ["I am proud to be a Dominican."]

For Sammy Sosa, that pride meant more than any award or record in baseball. He had returned to his country as a hero. But his journey to the top level of major league baseball had been long and hard.

HUMBLE BEGINNINGS

Sammy was born on November 12, 1968, in San Pedro de Macoris, in the Dominican Republic. He grew up in a square pink house with two rooms. He shared that tiny house with his mom, his four brothers, and his two sisters.

Sammy's father died when Sammy was 7. Sammy's mom was left to raise seven children by herself. Sammy and his brothers and sisters did whatever they could to help the family earn some money. Sammy sold oranges for 10 cents apiece on street corners and shined shoes for a quarter.

The national pastime

The Dominican Republic is an island country in the Caribbean Sea. It is a poor country, but it is rich in baseball talent. In 1999, 66 major league players were from the Dominican Republic. Ten of them were from San Pedro de Macoris. It's no wonder Sammy's hometown has been called the greatest baseball city in the world.

Dominican kids play baseball wherever they can: in the streets, in alleys, in sugarcane fields outside the city. Most kids dream of escaping the island's poverty by breaking into the major leagues. That's why Dominican players who make it to the majors are heroes to their countrymen. Sammy had to endure a childhood full of hardships before he would grow up to become like those heroes he worshipped.

An American friend helps out

When Sammy was 11, he and his brothers met an American businessman, Bill Chase. Mr. Chase had come to the Dominican Republic to open a shoe factory. Mr. Chase thought Sammy and his brothers were hardworking and polite. He let them shine his shoes and his customers' shoes to earn money. He allowed them to take showers in his factory. Soon Mr. Chase and his wife were buying clothes and food for the Sosas. The Sosa and Chase families grew very close.

Even though Sammy had to work, he found time to play baseball. Like most Dominican kids, he and his brothers and friends used bats made from guava-tree limbs, balled-up socks for balls, and milk cartons for gloves. They pretended to be the great players from the Dominican Republic who had made it to the major leagues, such as Hall of Fame pitcher Juan Marichal, who won 243 games in the 1960's, mostly for the San Francisco Giants.

When Sammy was 14, his older brother, Luis, got him involved in organized baseball. Sammy began playing in the leagues around San Pedro de Macoris, near his home. In place of a milk carton, he now had a real glove that Mr. Chase had bought for him.

A Dominican saying

One of Sammy's biggest faults as a young ballplayer was his impatience at the plate. He often swung at the first pitch. There is a Dominican saying: *You can't walk off the island.* It means players don't get to the majors by waiting for pitches and taking walks. They have to swing and hit to get noticed. Sammy felt pressure to get noticed, so he swung at everything. He was determined to hit the ball, no matter where it was pitched. Hitting the ball was the only way to make it to the major leagues and the majors meant big money. Sammy desperately needed money to help his family.

Sammy had a long way to go before he would develop the skills that have made him a star. Even so, at 15, he began showing signs of his raw power and hustle.

A year later, Sammy would get his chance to make a good impression on a major league scout. It would turn out to be the biggest break of his life, a major first step toward reaching his dream.

Sammy at age 12

THE FIRST STEPS TO STARDOM

Today, Sammy is a rock-solid 6 feet and 210 pounds. It's hard to imagine him as a 5' 10", 150-pound beanpole! But that's what he was when a Texas Ranger scout first saw him, in July 1985. Sammy was 16. The Rangers were one of several teams that sent scouts looking for talent in the Dominican Republic that summer. Ranger scout Omar Minaya invited Sammy and another kid to a field for the tryout. Sammy had borrowed a uniform and a pair of spikes with a hole in them for the tryout. Sammy's hustle was the first thing that caught Omar's eye.

"Because of the background that Sammy came from, he always needed to do everything right away," Omar remembers. "He needed to swing right away. When guys started running around the field, he was the first one, always. Sammy had a lot of pressure on him. He

knew that the survival of his family depended on him."

Omar saw that Sammy had a lot of potential. Even though Sammy wasn't particularly fast and his swing was unpolished, he had good bat speed and a strong throwing arm. He had the kind of power and strength that fire off home runs.

"In those days, we talked about Sammy Sosa being a 25-home-run guy," Omar said.

Early signs of a big-leaguer

On July 30, 1985, Omar gave Sammy $3,500 to sign a pro contract with the Rangers. That's not a lot of money, compared with the multi-millions Sammy earns today. But it was a fortune to Sammy back then. He gave most of the money to his mother but kept enough to buy himself a present: his first bicycle.

The Rangers didn't feel Sammy was quite ready to play on one of their minor league teams in the United States. They were worried that he and the other prospects from the Dominican Republic would have trouble adjusting to American culture. So they first sent them to a baseball academy in Santo Domingo, the capital of the Dominican Republic. Baseball academies are common in the Dominican Republic. At the academy, Sammy played baseball, studied English, and learned about the American culture.

When it was time for Sammy to board the plane that

would take him to his new home in the United States, the last thing he saw was when he looked over his shoulder was his mother. She was crying.

Sammy's destination was Sarasota, Florida, where he would join the the Rangers' Gulf Coast minor league team. Sammy looked like the most promising prospect on the team — until outfielder Juan Gonzalez arrived. Juan was from Puerto Rico, another island country in the Caribbean. Texas had given Juan a $75,000 bonus to sign.

Fast friends

Sammy and Juan were two of the best players on the team. They quickly became friends and developed a friendly rivalry. They both spoke Spanish and very little English, so they stuck close together.

"We stayed together all the time. We were roommates," Sammy said. "We cooked rice and beans. We had a good time. We both knew Spanish . . . so we had communication. That made it easy for us."

Said Juan: "We had the same dreams. We were working so hard. We were like a family."

There were times when not speaking English posed real challenges for Sammy and Juan. They once ate cat food by mistake because they couldn't read the label! They thought they were eating tuna fish, not tuna-flavored cat food! An American teammate had to translate the words on the label.

Sammy hit .275 in his first season with the Gulf Coast Rangers and led the league in doubles, with 19. He stole 11 bases but hit just four homers and struck out 51 times.

"I had a quick bat, but I didn't have the power and the discipline that I have right now," Sammy said. "I was an aggressive player who was going to go out there and swing at everything. *Boom, boom, boom!*"

Raw skills

Sammy's over-eager attitude also affected his defense. He played rightfield and was constantly overrunning the ball. He would charge grounders as if he were an infielder dashing in to field a bunt. Omar describes how Sammy "would sweep the ball, pick it up, throw it, and who knows where it was going to go? Most of the time he would sweep, look for the ball in his glove, and it wasn't there. So he'd go running back."

Pitcher Curt Schilling of the Philadelphia Phillies played for a Boston Red Sox minor league team in those days. He remembers watching Sammy play.

"He was a horrible outfielder," Curt said. "He was just absolutely as raw as you could be."

Former major leaguer and Dominican legend Felipe Alou was then managing the Montreal Expos' Gulf League team. When Felipe watched Sammy he saw in him the gifts that would make him a star. He believed Sammy would blossom and succeed in the major leagues someday.

"Even though Sosa was small, you could see the arm and the speed," Felipe said. "And when he made contact, the *power*."

That power would grow. And grow. And grow.

4

SAMMY GETS THE CALL

Sammy played 61 games in 1986 with the Gulf Coast Rangers before being promoted to their next minor league level. He joined the Gastonia Rangers of the Class A South Atlantic League at the start of the 1987 season. At Gastonia, Sammy got the experience he needed. He had twice as many at-bats and hit twice as many home runs as the season before. He even made the midseason South Atlantic League All-Star team.

But Sammy still hadn't learned an important lesson: patience. He struck out twice as often as the season before and rarely walked. He also made 17 fielding errors.

Sammy's coaches tried to slow him down. They tried to convince him not to swing at bad pitches and to play more cautiously on defense.

But Sammy felt he needed to get to the major leagues *quickly*. He didn't have time to take it slow. Back home, his mom had remarried, and his stepfather was very sick. Sammy sent them all the money he could.

The Rangers often sent Sammy's family extra money, thanks to Omar, the scout who had signed him. Omar and Sammy had become good friends. Omar had asked the Rangers to help out the Sosas from time to time.

"Sammy had a lot of pressure to succeed because his family's future depended on him," Omar said. "All the weight of the family was on his shoulders . . . My job a lot of the time with Sammy was to tone it down, [to tell him,] 'Let things come to you.' He was very receptive. But he was [still] going to do it his way."

Next stop: top of the minors

In 1988, the Rangers promoted Sammy to the Port Charlotte Rangers of the Florida State League, the highest Class A circuit. Once again, he improved in some categories but declined in others. For example, he led the league in triples but was caught stealing 24 times. The Rangers felt that if Sammy could ever improve *all* his stats, he would really be something special!

"You knew he was going to play in the big leagues," said Port Charlotte manager Bobby Jones. "His work ethic was outstanding. His hustle was outstanding. He was a hungry ballplayer and wanted it more than anybody else."

Sammy was *so* hungry and so eager to hit home runs

that he sometimes ignored his coaches' instructions. One time when Sammy was at the plate, Bobby Jones gave him the bunt sign. On the first pitch, Sammy swung away and hit a foul ball. Bobby gave Sammy the sign again. Sammy ignored him again and hit into a double play. When Sammy got back to the dugout, Bobby screamed at him in front of his teammates. Sammy was benched for three games and fined $25.

Some young players would have pouted. Not Sammy. He wasn't ashamed to admit his mistake. He apologized to Bobby the next day.

One year later, in 1989, Sammy was promoted to the Tulsa Drillers, the Rangers' Class AA team, in Tulsa, Oklahoma. It was expected to be the next step on his journey to the major leagues. Instead, it became a launching pad!

The majors, at last

Sixty-six games into the season in Tulsa, Sammy was hitting .297, with seven homers, 31 RBIs, and 15 doubles. Then he got The Call. The Rangers needed an outfielder to replace the injured Pete Incaviglia. They wanted Sammy. He was headed to the major leagues, the Big Show!

In the Tulsa clubhouse, Sammy's pal Juan Gonzalez joked that Sammy would be back in Tulsa as soon as Pete was healthy again. "I'll see you in 15 days," Juan told Sammy. "No," replied Sammy. "You're not going to see me

[back] here. I'm going to go up there and do my job. That's the chance that I need. That's the chance I've been looking for."

The call from Texas was thrilling, but there would be many more twists and turns on Sammy's ride to the top.

AT THE
BIG SHOW

Less than 24 hours after arriving in Texas, Sammy got his first taste of the big leagues. Starting for the Rangers, he had two hits in a June 16, 1989 game against the New York Yankees. The hits made a great first impression on his new teammates.

But the *big* test came five days later, at Fenway Park, in Boston, Massachusetts. Sammy faced Red Sox fireball pitcher Roger Clemens for the first time. The 6' 4" Roger was already a two-time Cy Young Award winner, and batters didn't look forward to facing his smoke! But Sammy passed the test with flying colors, hammering his first big-league homer. Sammy would look back on that game and tell the *The Dallas Morning News*, "From that day I said, 'I think I'll be a good player.'"

The Rangers believed Sammy would do well in Texas. "I thought he had the right attitude," said Bobby Valentine, the New York Met manager who was then managing the Rangers. "I thought he'd have decent long-ball potential. Not big power, but maybe around

15 to 20 homers [per season]."

Sammy got off to a good start with the Rangers, but then started to slide and fell into a slump. After 25 games, he was batting just .238. Unfortunately, he would have to return to the minors. The Rangers sent him to Oklahoma City to play for their their AAA club, the Oklahoma 89ers.

A tough lesson: the business of baseball

Back in Texas, the Rangers were battling for the American League West title. But they were missing something. Texas general manager Tom Grieve wanted to find one more big bat for the pennant chase. In July 1989, he started talking with the Chicago White Sox about a trade for big-hitting outfielder Harold Baines. They were interested, but they wanted too much for Harold. The Sox wanted either Sammy or Juan Gonzalez, plus a promising pitcher, in return for Harold. Tom said no.

In late July, White Sox general manager Larry Himes and two Sox scouts traveled to Oklahoma City to watch Sammy play. Sammy hit just .103 in 10 games, but the Sox liked what they saw. They wanted Sammy.

On July 29, Texas traded Sammy and two other players for Harold Baines and an infielder. "We like Sosa for his attitude, his hustle, and certainly his talent," Larry Himes said in *Sammy Sosa: Clearing the Vines*, a biography about Sammy by George Castle. "He is a

five-tool player: hit, hit for power, catch, run, and throw."

The trade was Sammy's first taste of the business side of baseball. It wouldn't be his last. It was bad enough that he was changing organizations. But what really made it tough was leaving his good friend Juan.

"I was feeling a little down [after the trade], because we were so close, such good friends," Sammy said. "I said, 'Okay, I just have to go to the other team' because I didn't have a choice."

The White Sox assigned Sammy to the Vancouver Canadians, their class AAA Pacific Coast League team, to give him some practice before joining the Sox. Sammy made quite a splash, hitting .367 in 13 games. That was good enough for the big club. On August 12, Sammy was called up to the White Sox.

The Sox were stuck in last place, but that didn't bother Sammy. He was happy to be back in the majors and eager to impress. He certainly didn't lack confidence: he told the club he could do *everything* in baseball.

Sammy backed up his big words. He had an amazing first game against the Minnesota Twins, smacking three hits in three at-bats including a two-run homer.

After playing in four different cities, Sammy played the rest of the 1989 season in Chicago. Said manager Jeff Torborg: "I took one look at him, and I said, 'There's our answer in rightfield.' He had a . . . terrific arm. And he showed respect and genuine sincerity. He was polite."

Sammy appeared to be anchored with the White Sox for 1990. He responded with a little bit of everything, as he had done time and again. He hit well but still fanned a lot. He finished second among American League outfielders with 14 assists, but he made 13 errors.

Sammy's free-swinging ways started to create

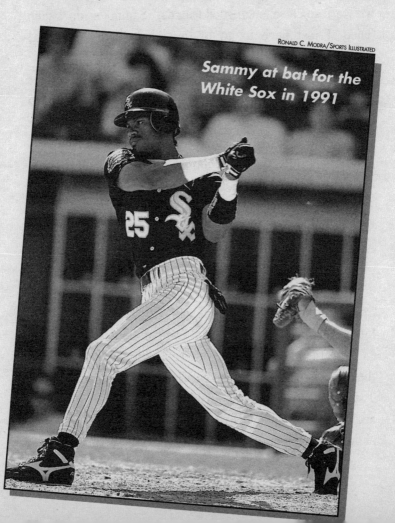

RONALD C. MODRA/SPORTS ILLUSTRATED

Sammy at bat for the White Sox in 1991

some tension among his White Sox teammates in 1990.

But Sammy's real trouble came from Sox hitting coach Walt Hriniak. Walt wanted players to make contact, not to swing for the fences. Though Sammy tried to work with Walt, the two didn't get along.

"Sammy was so strong, he had an uppercut swing," manager Jeff Torborg said in *Sammy Sosa: Clearing the Vines*. "He was such a gung-ho kid and wanted to do everything to please everyone. He tried to adapt to Walter's style, but it didn't fit him."

It appeared that Sammy was being *pushed* to fit in with Walter's style.

In 1992, Sammy would be pushed right out of a White Sox uniform. It would turn out to be the best thing that ever happened to him.

6

HELLO, WRIGLEY FIELD

Sammy started the 1991 season with a bang. But by July he was in a slump. Once again, the White Sox sent him down to the Vancouver Canadians. Sammy came back up on August 27 to finish the season with the Sox, but his future with the club was in doubt. White Sox general manager Larry Himes had been replaced by Ron Schueler. Ron wasn't a big fan of Sammy's.

"[Sammy had] all kinds of tools, things you're looking for in the perfect player, as a scout," said Ron in *Sammy Sosa: Clearing the Vines*. "But at that point in his career, he couldn't do anything to help you win a game. He'd throw to the wrong base, [make baserunning mistakes that would] run you out of an inning. You needed a walk, he'd swing at three pitches in the dirt . . . no discipline whatsoever. He wanted to swing like everything was going to be a home run. He did not try to get guys over [advance the base runners]."

The White Sox had run out of patience. Just days before the start of the 1992 season, Ron traded Sammy to the Chicago Cubs for slugging outfielder George Bell.

The Cubs were thrilled to have Sammy. They told him he would play every day. But Sammy still had a long way to go.

Bad breaks

Cub first baseman Mark Grace remembers his first impression of Sammy. "When he first got here, you could see he had great physical skills, but he was so raw," Mark told *Sports Illustrated*. "He didn't know how to play the game . . . . So many little things he just didn't know."

Because of bad luck, Sammy didn't get much of a chance to play. Injuries cut short his playing time in his first season as a Cub. On June 12, 1992, a pitch broke a bone in his right hand. He didn't play again until July 27. He returned in style and had a great first game back, hitting a homer in his first at-bat.

"I wanted to come back quick," Sammy said after the game. "I was excited about coming back, and I wanted to show what I could do, but I wanted to be patient [at the plate]."

Sammy hit .384 and thrilled the Cubs and their fans during his first nine games back. But Game 10 changed everything. He fouled a pitch off his right ankle, breaking the bone. It was the last game Sammy would play that season.

Still, he had found a home in the Windy City with his new team across town from the White Sox. The Cubs believed in Sammy and were committed to him.

By the following season, 1993, Sammy's anklebone had healed and he came roaring back.

Setting records has its price

Sammy would explode for 33 homers and 93 RBIs by the end of the season. On July 2, against the Rockies in Colorado, he went 6-for-6 and set a club record with nine straight hits (counting his hits in the previous game). Though he still struck out a lot, Sammy was growing as a player.

"Right now, I'm just being patient, more patient than I used to be," Sammy said after his big game against the Rockies.

Sammy set another club record that season. He became the first Cub to hit 30 homers and steal 30 bases. But with those records came criticism. Some people felt he was a selfish player. They thought he cared too much about setting records and trying to homer on every pitch and not enough about the team.

A *Chicago Tribune* reporter summed up the criticism in a story. He wrote: "The rap against Sosa, whispered by his teammates and occasionally spoken aloud by those outside the Cubs' organization, is that many of Sosa's statistics are selfish. That he will steal a base in a lopsided game solely to pad his numbers. Or

that he swings from his heels for a home run every time."

Sammy would answer his critics by reminding them of that Dominican baseball expression: *You can't walk off the island* (meaning, players don't get to the majors by taking walks; they have to hit.)

"It's not easy for a Latin player to take 100 walks," Sammy told *Sports Illustrated* in 1998. "If I knew the stuff I know now seven years ago — taking pitches, being more relaxed — I would have put up even better numbers. But people have to understand where you're coming from.

"When I was with the White Sox, [shortstop] Ozzie Guillen said to me, 'Why do you think about money so much?' I said, 'I've got to take care of my family.' And he told me, 'Don't think about money. Just go out and play, and the money will be there. It takes a while.' "

The big bucks

Since joining the Cubs in 1993, Sammy had hit 157 homers. In 1995, he tied for second in the National League in home runs and was selected to play in his first All-Star Game. He had his best home-run season in 1996, hitting 40.

In the middle of the 1997 season, the Cubs signed him to a four-year, $42.5 million contract. That shocked many baseball people. Sammy had played in one All-Star Game. He hadn't proved he could carry a team to the playoffs. The Cubs thought he could.

Chicago general manager Ed Lynch told *Sports Illustrated* what the Cubs saw in Sammy. "We saw a five-tool player who was coming into what are the prime years for most guys . . . We were banking that he would continue to improve."

In 1998, Sammy showed the world that the Cubs were right to believe in him. He did it in spectacular fashion.

7

A SEASON LIKE NO OTHER

Baseball needed Sammy and Mark McGwire in 1998. The players' strike of 1994-1995 was long over, but fans were still upset with players. Attendance at games was down in some cities. Television ratings fell. Many people had lost interest in baseball.

Then the long balls started flying over stadium fences, and all was forgiven!

The summer of 1998 will always be remembered for The Chase: Sammy and Mark were in a neck-and-neck race to break Roger Maris's single-season record of 61 homers. The record had stood for 37 years.

"It's excellent for the game," Mark said as The Chase raged through the summer. "It's fantastic. I totally realize that. I think everyone realizes the game is on an uprise now."

Few people were surprised that Mark, the St. Louis Cardinals' muscular first baseman, would make a run at 62 homers. Since entering the league with the Oakland A's, in

1986, he had hit 387 home runs. If he had not been injured for most of the 1993 and '94 seasons, he might have challenged the record earlier. Mark's size (6' 5", 250 pounds) and strength help him swing so fast that his bat appears to bend when it meets the ball! Mark didn't just hit homers, he crushed them. Balls left the park as if shot from a long-range cannon. The question wasn't *if* they would make it over the fence, but *how far* they would sail.

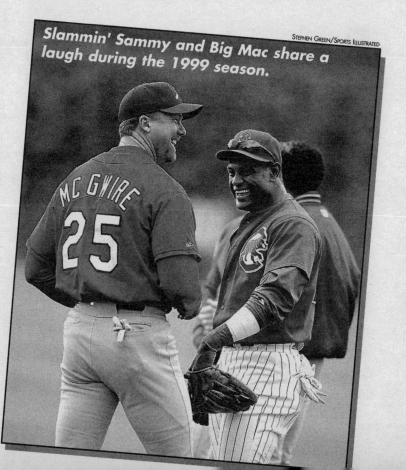

STEPHEN GREEN/SPORTS ILLUSTRATED

Slammin' Sammy and Big Mac share a laugh during the 1999 season.

It wasn't that way with Sammy. Sure, he had power and strength. But he had never hit a ball 517 feet, as Mark had in St. Louis's Busch Stadium in 1997. And though he had once hit 40 homers in a season, hitting 60 was another story.

Rewind! A videotape helps Sammy

As the 1998 season started, Sammy was ready for big things, thanks to Cub hitting coach Jeff Pentland. After the 1997 season, Jeff had sent the slugger home with a videotape of Sammy and two major leaguers: the Atlanta Braves' Chipper Jones and Chicago teammate Mark Grace.

Jeff pointed out how all three tapped their left foot on the ground before the pitch arrived. It was like a trigger to begin their swing. Chipper and Mark tapped their feet as the ball was halfway to the plate, but Sammy waited too long. By tapping earlier, Sammy could slow down and see pitches better. And if Sammy could see pitches better, he would be less likely to swing at a bad one.

Sammy also felt more relaxed in 1998 than he had the previous season, which helped his concentration. Signing the contract in 1997 had been a relief to Sammy, as it meant he could take care of his family. At the same time, Sammy felt pressure to prove he was worth that money.

"There was too much pressure [in 1997]," Sammy

told *Sports Illustrated* in June 1998. "Pressure from the contract, pressure to do it all. I felt if I didn't hit a home run, we wouldn't win. I was trying to hit two home runs in one at-bat. Now I don't feel that anymore."

As the 1998 season began, the videotape clearly had helped Sammy learn to see pitches better. He was waiting for a good pitch and chasing fewer sliders and curveballs. By the end of May, he had 13 homers, good for seventh in the National League. That was nice, but Mark had slugged his 25th on May 25.

Then came June . . . and the explosion.

Shhh! Whisperings of Sammy hitting 60!

Sammy went from power hitter to power source. In the first 21 days of June, he slammed 17 dingers to set a major league record for most home runs in one month. But he wasn't even through! By June 30, he had hit 20 homers. All of a sudden, there was talk of 60. And beyond.

"I've seen a lot of things in this game, but I've never seen anything like this," Mark Grace told *Sports Illustrated* about Sammy's explosion. "The game of baseball has never seen anything like it. I really don't have words for it."

Others offered their own explanations about Sammy's sensational burst.

"Sosa's scary, especially when he puts the ball in the air in [Wrigley Field]," Philadelphia Phillies manager Terry

Francona told *Sports Illustrated.* "He doesn't chase pitches the way he used to."

"He's not missing mistakes [by the pitchers]," Phillie catcher Mark Parent said. "That's the big thing for all good hitters — McGwire, [Ken] Griffey, and those guys. They don't swing at bad balls, and they hammer mistakes. They make you pay for every mistake. That's what Sammy's doing."

Sammy was thrilled with his big start, but he was embarrassed when people said he could hit 60 homers. "I'll just let you people [reporters] take care of that. I don't want you to put me in that kind of company [with Babe Ruth and Roger Maris]" Sammy told *Sports Illustrated.*

Sammy's play left reporters no choice but to keep asking about 60. A homer on July 31 against the Rockies gave him 42. You didn't have to be a math whiz to know he needed just 18 more to reach 60. The big question was: Who would get there first, Sammy or Mark?

The race heats up

Through August, the battle got more intense. Sammy took the lead on August 19, when he slugged his 48th homer against the Cardinals. Mark answered with a six-homer burst in the next five games to regain the top spot.

"He's the Man," Sammy said about his competitor. "He's the type who can hit five, six homers in a couple of

days. I put my money on him . . . I'm not thinking about the record. I'm . . . thinking about the game. If I think about the game, I'll play better."

Sammy *was* thinking about the game. The Cubs were in the race for the National League wild-card spot. But fans were into the home-run chase! When Sammy knocked numbers 50 and 51 out of Wrigley on August 23, Latin Americans rejoiced. He had become the first Latin player to reach the 50 mark. "I'm not going to lie to you," Sammy said. "I'm proud."

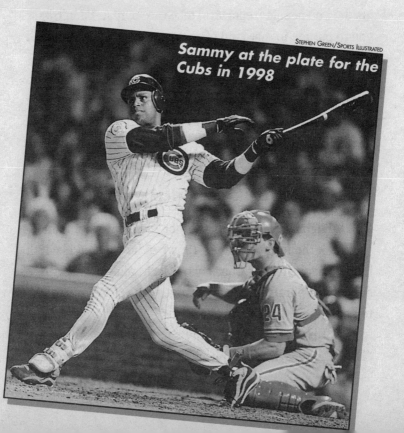

STEPHEN GREEN/SPORTS ILLUSTRATED

Sammy at the plate for the Cubs in 1998

The race continued into September. Mark hit his 60th on September 5. Sammy slugged number 58. Two days later, Mark hit Number 61 to tie Roger Maris. The next day, September 8, would go down in baseball history.

Big Mac hits number 62

Mark and the Cardinals were facing the Chicago Cubs in St. Louis, Missouri. In the fourth inning, Steve Trachsel threw Mark a fastball. With one mighty swing, Mark sent the ball flying. "I thought the ball was going to hit the wall," Mark later told reporters. "The next thing I know, it disappeared. What an incredible feeling. I did it!"

Steve Trachsel would later say this about the historic pitch: "The pitch was shin-high, off the inside corner. Maybe I will think about giving up the record-breaker after I retire. Right now, it's just another home run. I've given up a billion of them."

Sammy congratulated his friend Mark, as he had all season. After Mark hit the record-setting homer, Sammy leapt into Mark's arms. "When he hugged me, it was a great moment I am not going to forget," Sammy said.

Sammy tied — and surpassed — Roger on September 13 with two homers against the Milwaukee Brewers. He finished the year with 66, four behind Mark.

Mark finished the season with 70 home runs to

Sammy's 66. Their home-run race was just what baseball needed to draw fans back. Attendance at ballparks went up. TV sets were turned on everywhere as the country watched Sammy and Mark duel to the last. Baseball, America's pastime, was back!

And Sammy was no longer a wild swinger. He had become a superstar.

8

ENCORE! ENCORE!

Fans had been thrilled by the amazing home-run derby of 1998. They wanted a repeat performance in 1999! They were hoping for a home run every time Mark or Sammy stepped to the plate.

"Basically, the name of the game now is home runs," Sammy told reporters on September 19, 1999, after hitting his 61st home run for the second time in his career. "All the people come to the park to see us hit them. That was one of the reasons why Mark and I brought baseball back last year."

Yet, even after Sammy's amazing 1998 season, there were some people who still weren't convinced of his talent. Some doubters thought Sammy had homered a lot because there were a lot of average pitchers in the league (due to the increased number of baseball teams when the league started expanding.) Others said the major leagues were using "juiced" baseballs (balls with the yarn wrapped tighter than usual to make the ball harder. Harder balls travel farther). Major League Baseball denied this. Others said Sammy got lucky in 1998. He couldn't do it again.

Oh, yes, he could! After a slow start in April, Sammy

was back in rare form by the end of May. He cranked 13 homers and hit .321, earning the National League Player of the Month honor. He continued his rapid pace through June, when he parked 13 homers to close the month with an even 30.

Once again, the number 60 was on everyone's mind. Could Sammy do it for the second season in a row? It would be amazing, considering how slowly his career had begun. On June 26, Sammy hit the 300th homer of his career, launching a 465-foot missile to centerfield against the Philadelphia Phillies.

Instant replay: shooting for 60

By the All-Star break, Sammy led the major leagues with 32 homers. His friendliness and big smile had also made him a fan favorite. He received more All-Star votes than any other player.

Meanwhile, Mark McGwire was on a tear of his own. Mark had hit 28 homers by the All-Star break. By August 21, he had 47 and Sammy had hit number 51. Less than a month later, Sammy became the first player to hit 60 or more homers in two straight seasons. He hit number 60 in Milwaukee on September 18. Mark hit his 60th round-tripper eight days later.

Sammy would again lose the homer chase to Mark, this time by 65–63. But how could anyone doubt Sammy's talent now?

"I remember at the beginning of the year, a lot of people were saying it was impossible to happen two years in a row," Sammy said. "And here I am."

Sammy finished 1999 with a league-leading 89 extra-base hits. More important, he walked a career-high 78 times. Sure, he had whiffed 171 times, but who cared now?

"Nobody was thinking Mark and I would have had the opportunity to do it again," Sammy said on September 18. "You just never know in this game. Everything is possible. I have faith in my ability and my talent and all the work I put into it. That has made me come back and have another great year."

Sammy also won the first National League Hank Aaron Award. Players are given 1 point for each home run, hit, and RBI. The player with the most points wins the award. Sammy finished 17 points ahead of the second-place finisher.

A helping hand

Sammy felt that with all the good fortune he had in his baseball career, it was important for him to help people in need. In 1998, he started the Sammy Sosa Foundation. The foundation's main goal is to improve the health and education of children in the Dominican Republic. It has provided computers, books, and school supplies to Dominican children. In 1998, the foundation reached out to victims of Hurricane Georges, which had

devastated the Dominican Republic, by sending relief supplies.

In August 1999, the foundation announced the opening of the Sammy Sosa Childrens' Medical Center for Preventive Medicine, in San Pedro de Macoris. The center provides free vaccines to kids to protect them from disease.

Major League Baseball presented Sammy with the 1998 Roberto Clemente Man of the Year award. The award

RONALD C. MODRA/SPORTS ILLUSTRATED

Sammy fielding for the Cubs in 1999

is given each year to the player who best represents baseball, on and off the field. Roberto Clemente was a Pittsburgh Pirate legend. He died in a plane crash in 1972 while delivering relief supplies to earthquake victims in Nicaragua. Sammy wears number 21 on his jersey to honor Roberto, who also wore number 21.

A hero to many

Dominicans in the U.S. adore Sammy as much as Dominicans in his native country do. New York City has a large Dominican population. During the home-run chase of 1998, residents of the city's largest Dominican neighborhood kept a running total of Sammy's home runs. They wrote the home-run number on windshields, on homemade signs in windows, and on sidewalks. On summer nights when the Cubs were playing, cheering could be heard coming from apartment buildings every time Sammy hit a homer.

Fans love to watch Sammy, who always seems to be having fun when he plays. He often takes a playful hop when he begins his "home-run trot." When he comes to bat or when he runs out to take his spot in rightfield at the start of a game, the fans begin to chant his name.

"Sammy isn't just a great hitter," Cub first baseman Mark Grace says. "He always plays with a smile. He's fun to be around."

Off the field, Sammy says he has fun playing with his

dogs (he has six of them!) and listening to merengue and saxophonist Kenny G.

Best of all, Sammy likes just hanging out with his wife, Sonia, daughters Keysha and Kenia, and sons Michael and Sammy junior. Sammy says his favorite hobby is taking his kids to the amusement park.

Sammy's family back in the Dominican Republic is always in his heart, too. Sammy's mom watches the Cubs on TV back home. Every time Sammy hits a home run, he sends her a special message. He kisses two fingers, touches his heart, and blows a kiss. "It's my way of saying I love her," Sammy says. "My life is pretty much a miracle."

Dream big: Dreams can come true!

Sammy has always believed in himself, even when others didn't. His heart, determination, and hard work are the biggest reasons he has achieved everything he has today.

Sammy had come to the United States with nothing but a big dream 13 years earlier. He wanted to use his baseball skills to help his family out of poverty. He helped his family, and many, many others.

Sammy is considered one of baseball's greatest players. But he hasn't forgotten where he came from and how hard he had to work to get where he is. When he steps

up to the plate to bat, he is playing for an entire nation. When Dominican kids play ball, they dream of being the next Sammy Sosa.

After all, Sammy once had big dreams. Look how far those dreams took him!

WANT TO HAVE MORE FUN!

WITH SPORTS ILLUSTRATED FOR KIDS?

GET A FREE TRIAL ISSUE of SPORTS ILLUSTRATED FOR KIDS magazine. Each monthly issue is jam-packed with awesome athletes, super-sized photos, cool sports facts, comics, games, and jokes!

Ask your mom or dad to call and order your free trial issue today! The phone number is 1-800-732-5080.

PLUG IN TO www.sikids.com. That's the S.I. FOR KIDS website on the Internet. You'll find great games, free fantasy leagues, sports news, trivia quizzes, and more.

CHECK OUT S.I. FOR KIDS Weekly in the comic section of many newspapers. It has lots of cool photos, stories, and puzzles from the Number 1 sports magazine for kids!

LOOK FOR more S.I. FOR KIDS books. They make reading **fun!**